Meet the Werewolf

by Georgess McHargue

Drawings by Stephen Gammell

J.B.LIPPINCOTT COMPANY   Philadelphia and New York

This book is for Traci,
even though she has now given up
werewolves for dolphins.

Pictures appearing on page 14 courtesy of Culver Pictures, Inc.; page 23 courtesy of Mike Busselle, © Aldus Books Limited, London; page 34 by permission of University Books, Inc., Secaucus, New Jersey; pages 40, 41, 60, 63 courtesy of the New York Public Library Picture Collection. Jacket illustration by permission of University Books, Inc., Secaucus, New Jersey.

U.S. Library of Congress Cataloging in Publication Data

McHargue, Georgess.
    Meet the werewolf.

    Includes index.
    SUMMARY: The origins, habits, myths, legends, and famous case histories of werewolves.
    1. Werewolves—Juvenile literature. [1. Werewolves] I. Title.
GR830.W4M34   398′.469   75-34046
ISBN-0-397-31662-3   ISBN-0-397-31663-1 (pbk.)

Meet the Werewolf

Other titles in THE EERIE SERIES

GHOSTS
by Seymour Simon

MOVIE MONSTERS
by Thomas G. Aylesworth

WARNING

This is a scary book. Werewolves are supposed to be monsters that eat people, and it is impossible to write about them without some blood and gore. So if you like monsters and enjoy being a little scared, read on. But if you don't like the dark and always think something is looking in your window, this may not be the book for you.

Contents

Les Lupins *by Maurice Sand: a nighttime gathering of French werewolves*

1

What Is a Werewolf?

Old tales and legends say that there are people who sometimes turn into wolves. Sometimes they look like tall, hairy human beings with fierce wolves' heads. Sometimes they are wolves with human faces. But most often they simply turn into extra-large, terrifying wolves, many times stronger and more cunning than ordinary wolves. In wolf form they run through the town or countryside, killing and eating any living thing they meet. They are especially fond of cattle, sheep, and human beings as food. And it is almost impossible to catch them. They have the brains of human beings as well as the strength and speed of wolves.

In their human form, most werewolves are cruel and angry people, although almost anyone *may* be a werewolf. There are even some friendly werewolves, and some who have become werewolves against their will.

The word *werewolf* is quite old. Most experts think it comes from the Old English *wer,* meaning man, and *wulf,* meaning, of course, wolf. Thus, a werewolf is a man-wolf or a man who can change into a wolf. By the way, the word should be pronounced to rhyme with "dear wolf," not with "her wolf."

In eastern and western Europe, people have believed in werewolves for more than two thousand years. One of the oldest werewolf stories ever written down appears in a book by a witty Roman writer named Petronius Arbiter, who died in A.D. 66. A man named Niceros was invited to a dinner party and told this tale to the other guests.

Niceros was in love with a pretty widow named Melissa who lived outside the town. One evening Niceros set out to visit her. He persuaded a young soldier to keep him company on the road, and they set off together.

There were gravestones on either side of the highroad, but Niceros sang cheerfully to himself in the bright moonlight and counted the stars overhead. Suddenly, something made him turn around. He saw that the soldier had stopped by the side of the road. As Niceros watched, he took off all his clothes, made a magic circle around them, and turned into a wolf. The wolf gave a howl and ran off into the woods.

Poor Niceros was left with shaking knees in the roadway. At last he dared to go over and look at the soldier's clothes. To his terror, he saw that they had been turned to stone. Pale and trembling, he made his way to his sweetheart's house.

He found the place in an uproar. "If you had only been a little earlier," Melissa told him, "we could have used your help. A huge wolf broke in and attacked the farm animals. But he didn't get away with it completely. One of the farmhands gave him a good cut on the neck."

Niceros, naturally, was amazed at all this. He hurried home the next day to tell his adventure. When he came to the place where he had left the pile of clothes-turned-to-stone, he found only a pool of blood. And when he reached his house, he learned that the soldier was in bed suffering from a deep wound on the neck. "Then," adds Niceros, "I knew that he was a werewolf. After that, you could have killed me before I'd sit down to eat with him. Yes, and you may all think what you like of my story, but never have I told a word of a lie."

2

How to Tell a Werewolf When You See One

Almost anyone may be a werewolf. Men, women, and children, peasants and noblemen, beggars and businessmen, young and old, every group contains werewolves. Some werewolves in their human form are fierce and frightening-looking, but some look just like your next-door neighbors, your classmates, and the people you meet on the bus.

There may even have been at least one king who was a werewolf. King John of England (died 1216) was most unpopular during his lifetime and after his death there were some who swore he had become a werewolf—as cruel and greedy as he had been in life.

Still, there are some small ways that most werewolves are alike. Or so say those who claim to have seen them.

15

If you are wondering whether a person is a werewolf, look first at the eyebrows. If they meet in a point over the nose, chances are good that the person is a werewolf.

What about the teeth? They may be beautiful, and white. But are they just a little longer and more pointed than usual? Some werewolves may even have teeth that are black or reddish in color.

Next, look at the hands. If the first, or index, finger is as long as the second, or middle, finger, it may be a sign of werewolfery. Most important, is there hair on the palms of the hands? Are the hands broad and the fingers short? Are the fingernails long and curving?

Are the ears set very low and far back on the head?

Werewolves often like their meat rare, or even eat it raw. Like some other people (the author is one), they don't like to eat their vegetables.

Werewolves are pale, their eyes and mouths are dry, and they are always thirsty. They hate bright light and will keep to dark and shady places as much as possible.

Another important sign is that werewolves are often covered with the thorn scratches and dog bites they get while running in wolf form. Any wounds a werewolf receives in wolf form will always be found on his body in human form also. Many werewolves are discovered in this way.

There are many stories that go something like this. A farmer was coming home from market to his lonely cottage in the hills when he was attacked by an enormous wolf. The farmer, however, was a strong and stout man. After a great struggle, he managed to pull out his knife and hack off the wolf's left forepaw. The animal then limped off howling, and the man made his way home. Full of his adventure, he burst into the house and began to tell his wife what had happened. Only when he was halfway through the story did he see the bloody rags wrapped around the place where his wife's left hand should have been.

It is also said that the time when werewolves are most likely to prowl is either in the month of February or on Christmas. In Scandinavia, werewolves gather together on Christmas. They break into ale-houses and drink all the beer they can find.

3

How to Become a
Werewolf

The person who wishes to become a werewolf has a choice of several ways of doing it. Some would-be werewolves must first make a pact with the Devil. The reason is the old belief that all magic comes from the Devil. Anyone who wanted special powers could arrange to get them from the Devil just the way you might buy an automobile from a dealer. But the Devil was a very clever salesman, and the price he usually asked was the buyer's soul. Not everyone believes in the Devil, but those who do agree that it is not a good idea to have anything to do with him.

Still, there have always been people who thought they could cheat the Devil and get what they wanted without losing their souls. The simplest way to make a werewolf pact was just to wish very hard to be a werewolf and to call on the Devil for help. The Devil

18

might appear as a man dressed all in black or as a horrible demon. He would then give the would-be werewolf a mysterious belt made either of wolf skin or of human skin. The person who put it on could turn into a wolf at will.

In Belgium, they tell the tale of a young man and his sweetheart who went out walking on the sand dunes by the sea. There they came across an odd-looking belt made of braided black hair and fastened with a beautiful gold buckle. The boy picked it up, intending to give it to his girl for a present. She, however, turned pale and refused to touch it.

"Very well," said the boy, trying to hide his hurt feelings. "If you don't want it, I'll give it to Nippo."

The devil makes his mark on three persons as a sign of the pact between them. Often these pacts involve werewolfery.

He called to his dog Nippo, who came bounding up. But as soon as the belt had been fastened around the dog's neck, a terrible change took place. The friendly house dog was turned into a huge black wolf. With a flash of red eyes and an evil snarl, the beast sprang at the boy. It might have killed him. But his true love bravely threw herself on the monster and removed the fatal belt. As soon as she did so, there was Nippo again. The dog wagged his tail and looked quite confused by the fuss. Warned by their experience, the couple burned the belt, which caused no more trouble.

Sometimes, instead of a belt, the Devil gives the werewolf a pot of ointment or salve, with which he is to rub himself whenever he wants to change into wolf form. Or the would-be werewolf may make the salve himself. This is probably the surest way to become a werewolf: On a night of the new moon, go to a lonely place such as a desert or mountaintop. Find a level spot (this may be hard, on a mountain). Draw on it with chalk a circle about seven feet across. Inside that, make another circle about three feet across. Then build a fire in the center of the small circle. Over the fire hang an iron pot from an iron stand. The pot and stand must be *iron*. Fill the pot with water, and bring it to a boil. Then throw in handfuls of any three of the following: parsley, hemlock, henbane, saffron, aloe, poppyseed, opium, solanum, and asafetida. Henbane and solanum are poisonous plants. Asafetida is a gummy, bad-smelling stuff made from the roots of several plants. Opium is a drug made from poppies. It is illegal to possess it in many countries.

One writer says that this is the spell that must then be recited:

> Spirits of the deep
> Who never sleep,
> Be kind to me.
>
> Spirits from the grave
> Without a soul to save,
> Be kind to me.
>
> Spirits of the trees
> That grow upon the leas,
> Be kind to me.
>
> Spirits of the air
> Foul and dark, not fair,
> Be kind to me.
>
> Spirits of the dead
> That glide with noiseless tread,
> Be kind to me.

Wolves, vampires, satyrs, ghosts!
Chosen of all the hateful hosts!
I pray you send hither,
Hither, hither,
That great gray shape that makes men shiver.
Shiver, shiver, shiver!
Come, come, come!

After repeating the spell, rub yourself with lard or some other kind of animal fat mixed with camphor, anise, and opium. Tie on a belt made of wolf skin. Finally, kneel down inside the large circle, *but outside the small circle.* This is important, because if you are inside the small circle, you may be snatched away by spirits.

If the spell has been said properly, and everything else has been done right, SOMETHING will then appear inside the inner circle. This something

This would-be werewolf has put herbs and drugs into a boiling pot, recited a spell, and rubbed himself with ointment. Now, with a wolf skin belt around his waist, he kneels in the magic circle and waits for a demon to give him the power to turn into a werewolf.

(whether it is a spirit or a demon) may give you the power to become a werewolf. At least, so it was widely believed throughout Europe for hundreds of years.

There are other ways of becoming a werewolf that are less trouble, but probably do not work so well. In the Harz Mountain section of Germany and in a few other places, for example, there were supposed to be werewolf streams. These little mountain brooks smelled and tasted strangely different from other streams. A drink of their water would turn the drinker into a werewolf, whether he wanted to be one or not. The same thing might happen to a person who drank water that had collected in a wolf's footprint, or so they said in Serbia and other parts of eastern Europe. An even surer way is to be bitten by a werewolf. (That is, if the victim is not eaten up on the spot.)

One of the most interesting and least-known ways of becoming a werewolf is to find and pick a certain kind of flower. This flower is supposed to grow in the Balkan region of southern Europe, but no one seems to agree on what it looks like. Some say it is like a yellow snapdragon (which sounds like the American wildflower we call butter-and-eggs).

Others say it is like a large red daisy or like a dead-white sunflower with a sickly smell. Whatever the flower may look like, all agree that it is very attractive. There are several stories of small children who went out picking flowers one summer day and came back as wolves to eat up their brothers and sisters and even their parents.

Finally, there are some people who are born werewolves or who become werewolves through no fault of their own. Usually, this is because they are under some sort of curse. In both Greece and Ireland, there are ancient tales of werewolf families. Each member of the family was doomed to spend nine years in wolf form. On the fatal day, the person would go to a certain pool in the forest, hang his or her clothes on a tree branch, and jump into the water. A wolf would come out of the water on the pond's farther shore and vanish into the woods. The wolf would return nine years later to the day, jump into the pond, and come out in proper human form, only looking nine years older.

In Sicily, they say that a child conceived at the new moon or a man who sleeps out in moonlight will become a werewolf.

It is also said that there are certain things that attract werewolves. Among these are marigolds, lilies-of-the-valley, and azaleas. Another is diamonds. One might think that the people most bothered by were-wolves would be very rich gardeners.

How to Get Rid of a Werewolf

As we have seen, there are a good many ways to become a werewolf. However, there are not nearly so many ways to get rid of a werewolf. Werewolves, especially in their wolf shape, are almost impossible to kill. They are not really immortal (as vampires are). But they are strong and fierce and cunning, and they can run tremendously fast.

Many people think that werewolves can be killed with a silver bullet, but that is not so. It is vampires that can't stand silver bullets. Werewolves just laugh at them.

In some stories, werewolves turn back into their human forms if they are wounded in a fight. This is not always the case. It is certainly not safe to get into a fight with a werewolf in hopes of making him go back to human form.

Of course, it is true that if anyone steals a werewolf's clothes while he is in wolf form, he will not be able to change back again. But that is not very helpful, since it would be much better to keep him from taking on the wolf form in the first place.

A somewhat better method is to make three cuts with a knife on the werewolf's forehead. This almost always works, if you can make him hold still long enough.

Even stranger is the cure described in the following story from Denmark.

There was a young man named Peter Andersen, whose family had all been werewolves for many centuries. Peter fell in love with a lovely girl named Elisa but was afraid to tell her he was a werewolf. Elisa returned Peter's love, for he was a good, honest young man, and soon they were married.

All went well for a while, until one day the young couple went to a local fair. There they enjoyed themselves so much that it was growing late when they set out in their wagon for home. As they rode through the moonlit forests and fields, Peter began to have his "wolf feeling." He knew that the dreaded change was about to take place.

Jumping down from the wagon seat, he said to his wife, "My darling, if anything comes toward you from the woods, do not be afraid, and do not hurt it. Only strike it with your apron, and all will be well."

Then he ran off into the trees, leaving poor Elisa very much surprised and alarmed.

When she had driven only a few hundred yards farther, a great gray wolf sprang at her out of the forest with white fangs flashing. Elisa was a brave girl and an intelligent one. She remembered what

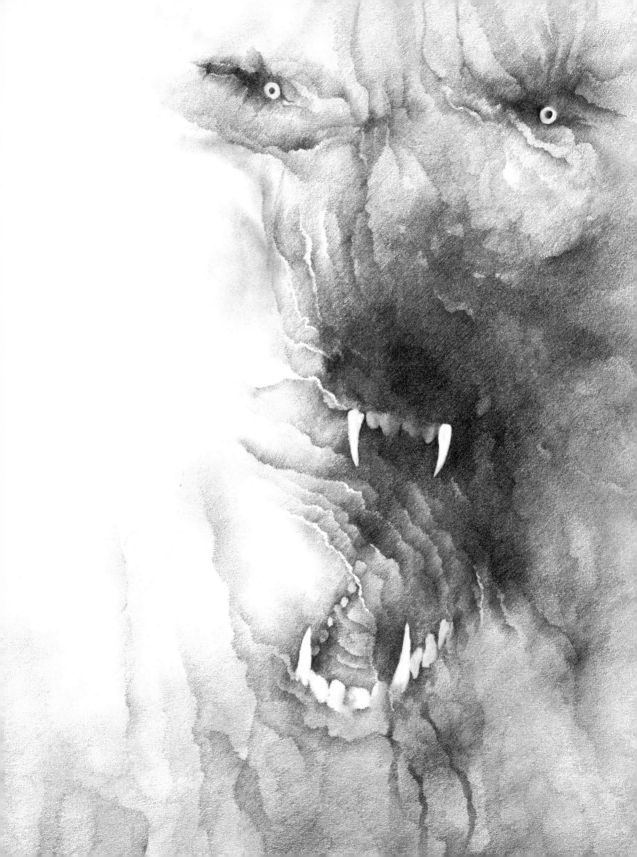

her husband had told her. Instead of screaming and trying to run, she ripped off her apron and flapped it in the beast's face. The wolf did not attack her, but merely tore the apron from her hand and ran off into the trees.

Elisa was still getting over her fright when her own dear Peter came out of the woods, holding her apron in his hand.

"Alas," she cried, "how can this have happened to me? How can the man I love be a werewolf?"

"I *was* a werewolf," admitted Peter, smiling, "but I am one no longer. You have saved me from this horrible curse by your bravery. Never again will I be forced to run on four feet howling like an animal." So Elisa forgave him for his secret, and they lived together happily for many years.

In some other stories, different pieces of clothing are thrown at the werewolf, such as hats and jackets. But this way of getting rid of a werewolf only seems to work when the werewolf *wants* to be cured. (The kind of werewolf who is under a curse often hates being a werewolf and wishes only to be like other people.)

To cure a werewolf who *likes* being a werewolf is another thing altogether. First, you have to catch the werewolf. This is easier when he or she is in human form. The werewolf must then be tied up. The best time to do this is on the night of the full moon. Then take the werewolf to a lonely spot.

From this point on, the spell for curing a werewolf is somewhat like the one for *becoming* a werewolf. First you draw a circle on the ground about seven feet across and put the werewolf in the middle of it. Then three girls must come forward and strike the werewolf with twigs from an ash tree. (Ash trees are often believed to be magic trees that keep away witches and other evil beings.) While they are hitting the werewolf, the three girls must chant:

> Graywolf ugly, graywolf old,
> Do at once as you are told.
> Leave this man and fly away—
> Right away, far away,
> Where it's night and never day.

Next the oldest person present must come up and give the werewolf a good, sound kick and say:

> Go, fly, away to the sky.
> Devilish graywolf, we do thee defy.
> Out, out, out, with a howl and a yell
> That will carry you faster and surer to hell.

Then the whole crowd must dip cups in a potful of hot liquid made from the following: sulphur, tar, vinegar, and castoreum. This hot, bad-smelling goo must be poured on the werewolf while everyone shouts and yells, urging him or her to go away and never come back. If the spell has been performed properly, the werewolf should turn back to a normal human being and will probably be very grateful to those who have done the cure.

Unfortunately, none of these cures is very useful if a werewolf attacks you suddenly. In that case, there are only two things you can do that offer much hope. One is to climb an ash tree. As I mentioned before, ash trees were thought to keep away witches, and it seems a werewolf won't go near one either. For some reason, werewolves also hate the kind of grain called rye. Several people have escaped from them by running into rye fields, or even by hiding in barns where rye straw was stored. Some say werewolves also dislike mistletoe, but I have never heard of anyone who escaped from a werewolf by use of this magic plant.

This picture by Laurence Housman shows a sleeper's nightmare about becoming an animal. Rituals connected with shape-shifting often involved a wolf skin.

5

Relatives of the Werewolf

As I said at the beginning, wolves are not the only creatures in folklore into which human beings may be changed. Many peoples the world over have believed in shape-shifting, as it is called.

Perhaps the oldest shape-shifters known are the Indian swan-maidens. They are beautiful girls, long-necked and graceful, who fly down to clear lakes in the form of swans. There they take off their "swan dresses" of feathers in order to bathe in the water. There are many tales, from India to Ireland, of the young man who falls in love with a swan-maiden and steals her swan dress. This, like stealing a werewolf's human clothing, prevents her from changing back into bird form. Young men sometimes marry swan-maidens and live happily for years. But it is a sad day if such a wife ever finds her stolen feather dress.

Then she will fly off as a swan to join her sisters and the human world will never see her again.

In the north of Scotland and Ireland, and on the coasts of Norway, people tell tales of the selchies (pronounced *sel*-kees), or seal folk. Like the swan maidens, the selchies are gentle and peace-loving. Their great sorrow is the cruel hunting of their brother seals by men.

> I am a man upon the land,
> I am a selchie in the sea,
> And when I'm far from every strand
> My home it is in Sule Skerry.

So says an old song from the area. Sule Skerry is indeed a rock in the Atlantic Ocean about fifty miles from the Orkney Islands, and just the sort of place a seal would like. Selchies live in great air-filled caverns under the sea, and there, also, they take human form.

Selchies sometimes marry human beings, but such marriages often end tragically. In the song from which I just quoted, for example, the selchie leaves his wife and baby, saying that the girl must not weep, for she will marry again. He also promises to come for his son when he is old enough to be taught selchie ways and "how to swim in the foam."

And indeed, the selchie comes for his son as promised. Then, the song says of the wife:

> She has married a gunner good,
> And a right fine gunner, I'm sure, was he.
> And he went out on a May morning,
> And shot the son and the gray selchie.

For, of course, it is a gunner's job in those parts to harpoon seals, and all seals look alike in the water. One can never know which are selchies.

In Japan, the chief shape-shifters are badgers and foxes. They often play tricks on human beings or other animals but are not really dangerous. The badgers, especially, can turn themselves into several other things besides human beings. In one story, a badger was grateful to a woodsman who had saved its life. It then turned itself into a valuable teakettle, which the woodsman was able to sell to a priest in the temple. However, the badger found it couldn't bear life as a kettle because polishing tickled it so much. (The priests weren't happy with it either, because it jumped and squeaked when handled roughly.) The badger therefore ran away back to the woodsman and became a dancing girl, whose dances made much money for the woodsman. At last, the life of a dancing girl became too tiring for the

A gathering of Japanese were-foxes in a lonely swamp

badger. It turned itself into a horse, hoping that its master could make money by renting it. However, and sad to say, the badger soon died of overwork. Though it had the form of a horse, it still had only the strength of a badger.

Another kind of shape-shifting, much more like the werewolves', is that of a berserker. In the tales and myths of Scandinavians, the berserkers were a group of terrible warriors who could take on the shape of bears in battle. In some of the tales, however, the berserkers are merely men who work themselves up into superhuman rages before going out to fight. They howl, foam at the mouth, and even bite through the edges of their iron shields, but they remain human beings. That is probably the clue to the way the whole story got started. If we look at the word *berserk,* we find that it means bear-sark, or bear-shirt. What is more natural than that in those cold places a group of warriors should go about dressed in the skins of bears? Bearskins would both keep them warm and frighten their enemies. Some scholars even think the berserkers took certain drugs before battle in order to work up their amazing rages. Whether or not that is so, it is easy to see how the bear-shirt men got the reputation of being half man, half bear.

The painter George Catlin here shows a group of Sioux Indians dancing in bear costumes. We do not know if the ancient berserkers had the same beliefs about bears, but perhaps they both admired the bear's strength and courage.

It would be useful if we could uncover something so simple behind the werewolf, but no one has so far done so. The werewolf stories are too widespread, and we do not know of any group of people who wore wolf skins to account for them.

Tales very much like those of the werewolf are told the world around, about whatever large, fierce animal happens to live in the neighborhood. There are were-tigers in India, where tigers may have the souls of the dead who are being punished for evil deeds. In Africa, there are both were-leopards and were-hyenas, but strangely no were-lions as far as I know. And in South America, there are were-jaguars. Often in the African and South American stories, the power of shape-shifting is a gift from some god or spirit and is for the purpose of getting revenge. Were-jaguars, were-leopards, and so on do not go around killing for pleasure. They only attack those who have done them wrong in their human form. Nevertheless, I'm not sure I would want to meet one of them on a dark night.

Jaguar heads like this ancient one from Central America often have human bodies. They are found all over Central and South America on statues, cloth, buildings, bowls, dishes, and jewelry.

Here is a tale about were-jaguars that takes place in the jungles of South America.

A Dutch trader named Van Hielen once went on business to an out-of-the-way Indian village. It was a fine evening and he was a man who liked nature. He thought he would take a walk toward the forest.

At the very edge of the clearing, far away from the village itself, Van Hielen found a lonely little hut. He was just wondering who would wish to live in such a spot when he heard shouts of anger and the sound of blows from inside the hut. Suddenly, a boy about eight or nine years old ran out the door. He was followed by a great fat woman who was hitting him cruelly with a piece of wood. The trader was fond of children and spoke the native language well. He stepped up to the woman and asked what the boy could have done to deserve such a beating.

"Done?" cried the woman. "Why, he has done nothing. That's why I beat him, the lazy lout. Not a stroke of work will he do. His sister is just as bad. Ah!" she broke off. "There's the wretched child now. She too will get what she deserves."

With that, the fat woman lunged for a thin girl of about ten who had come running from the forest at the sound of her brother's cries. Van Hielen was so upset at the sight of the heavy club raised against the two children that he hastily offered the woman money if she would let them alone. She snatched the coins greedily and disappeared into the hut with a last glare at the children.

"Poor things!" said the trader aloud. "How can a mother be so cruel to her own children?"

"Oh, but sir," exclaimed the little girl, "she is not our mother. She only makes us be her servants. You are kind, but do not trouble yourself. My name is Yaranka. My brother and I are the true children of the Forest Spirit, and she will help us to our revenge. We have suffered enough from that woman. We will get help from our true mother tonight in the Secret Place." With this speech, the two children made for the forest, leaving Van Hielen very much amazed.

That evening, the trader found he could not sleep for thinking of his strange experience. Quietly, he got up. He was determined to see what he could discover about these two children and their "mother." Keeping to the shadows, for the moon was bright, he hid himself near the hut. He could hear the loud snores of the fat woman. Not long after, he saw two small shadows creep from the hut and into the forest.

Van Hielen followed them, thankful that his many years in the country had taught him how to move silently through the jungle at night. Even so, he nearly lost sight of the two children many times.

They seemed to slip through the tangle of vines and bushes like elves.

After some time, they came to a small jungle clearing where a waterfall plunged into a pool in a shower of silver. In the center of the pool grew a single large and beautiful white water lily. Van Hielen hid himself behind a huge tree trunk. He was partly curious and partly worried about the safety of such young children in the dangerous forest at night. Yaranka and her brother seemed quite unworried, however. They knelt down by the edge of the water and began to chant in a language that Van Hielen had never heard before. At the end of the long chant, the children picked flowers from the bank and tossed them into the water.

The motion of the tossed flowers began to make the trader dizzy. The clearing seemed to be spinning around, with the children at its center. The rush of the waterfall was joined by the rush of a strange dark wind. Out of the earth, a vast figure reared itself. It was shapeless, towering, fearsome. Van Hielen clutched at the tree trunk with trembling hands. Then, in a mere flick of time, the figure vanished, the sickening motion of the clearing stopped, and all was as it had been before. Except—except that where the two children had stood, there now stood a pair of large jaguars. They were so close to him that he could count the spots on the sleek heads and even the whiskers on the snarling lips.

Van Hielen was a brave man, but he knew he had no chance against two such ferocious hunters at such short range. He saw the two pairs of green eyes gleam as the beasts scented him. He hoped only that his death would be quick. But suddenly one jaguar checked its leap and shouldered the other one aside also. The two furred bodies rushed silently past him on the narrow trail, so near that he could feel their hot breath. Then they were gone.

Very much shaken, Van Hielen pulled himself together and made his way back toward the village. He arrived at the edge of the clearing just as dawn was breaking. Everything appeared as usual—the doors of the huts were closed, the morning fires not yet lit. But as he passed the home of the fat woman, Van Hielen stopped dead. Leading straight to the door were the paw prints of two large jaguars. And from within the hut came the most horrible sound he had ever heard. It was a soft *crunch, crunch, crunch,* as if some large animal (or animals?) were gnawing on bones.

Without a backward glance, Van Hielen hurried on into the village. He did not want to open the door of the hut. He only felt quite sure that the two children would never be beaten by the fat woman again.

6

Jean Grenier, the Original "Teenage Werewolf"

So far, we have talked about legends and stories of werewolves. Now it is time to meet some of the werewolves, or supposed werewolves, in history.

In the spring of the year 1603, strange and terrible things began to happen in a certain district in the southwest of France. Children of all ages disappeared from roads and fields and were never seen

again. In one case, a baby vanished from its cradle. The people of the country began to mutter about wolves. Some hinted darkly at something worse than wolves. Everyone went in fear. Parents refused to let their children play more than a few yards from their doorsteps.

Then a girl named Marguerite Poirier (Pwar-*yay*), aged thirteen, came home with a startling story. One noonday, she said, she had been out watching the cattle. A beast like a huge dog with reddish fur rushed out of the bushes and attacked her. She was only able to save herself from being bitten because she had a strong stick with an iron point on it. The beast ran off. But later she met a boy named Jean Grenier (Jong Gren-*yay*) who boasted that he had been the wolf and that he would have eaten Marguerite if she hadn't hit him with her stick.

Next an eighteen-year-old girl named Jeanne Gaboriaut (Junn Ga-*bo*-ree-*oh*) came forward to tell what had happened to her. She and several other girls had been out watching cattle. Their herd dogs began to whine and growl at something down in a hollow of the ground. When the girls went to see what it was, they found a strange-looking boy of about thirteen. He was dirty, red-haired, and wild. His bushy eyebrows met in a point above his nose.

Jeanne asked him why he looked so odd, and the boy replied, "Ah, that is because I sometimes wear a wolf's skin." Horrified, Jeanne asked him what he meant. He told her that a man named Pierre Labourat (La-boo-*ra*) had given him a wolf skin. When he put it on, he turned into a wolf. In wolf shape, he boasted, he had hunted the entire district. Though he had killed and eaten many dogs, they were not as tasty as children. Quite naturally, the girls ran away to tell what they had heard.

A search was made for the boy called Jean Grenier. He was found and arrested. Quite willingly, he told the following story. He came from the tiny village of Saint' Antoine de Pizon. He had run away from home because his father beat him. Since then, he had made his living by herding cattle and begging.

One evening about three years before, another boy had taken him deep into the forest. There they met the Lord of the Forest, a tall man dressed in black, who rode a black horse. Jean met the Lord of the Forest several times afterward and agreed to be his servant. The Lord treated them well and gave them wine to drink, but he made a mark on each of them with his dagger. He also gave them each a wolf skin and some ointment. He told them to rub them-

selves with the ointment each time they wanted to put on the wolf skins and become wolves. The Lord told Jean that he must never cut the nail of his left thumb. and it had grown horny and crooked like a claw.

Jean gave a complete list of all the children whom he had killed and eaten since that time. He seemed proud of his deeds.

Many witnesses came forward to say that his story was correct. The court judged that Jean Grenier was a werewolf. He was sentenced to be shut up for life in a monastery (the home of a group of monks). In doing so, the court showed much more mercy than was usual at the time, for werewolves were generally sentenced to death.

7

Gilles Garnier, the Werewolf of Dôle

In the fall of 1572, near the French city of Dôle, the local Court of Parliament passed a law permitting the people of the district to hunt werewolves even though it was not the regular hunting season. The reason was that there had "often been seen and met, for some time past, a Were-wolf, who, it is said, has already seized and carried off several little children, so that they have not been seen since. . . . He has attacked and done injury in the country to some horsemen, who kept him off only with great difficulty and danger to their persons."

The hunt began. Although the disappearances went on, no sign of the werewolf was found for several weeks. One day, however, some peasants were passing through a forest and heard screams for help. They ran toward the sounds and found a little girl

defending herself bravely against a monstrous wolf which had already bitten her in five places. The men soon drove the beast off. It loped into the gloom of the underbrush. Some of the men thought what they saw was not a wolf but an old man known as the Hermit of St. Bonnot (San Bon-*no*).

In spite of their suspicions, nothing was done until six days later, when a ten-year-old boy was reported missing from a place near the Hermit's hut.

The Hermit was then brought in for questioning. He was an old man with a long beard, a pale face, burning eyes, and bushy eyebrows that met in a point over his nose. His name was Gilles Garnier (Jeel Garn-*yay*). He confessed that, like Jean Grenier and others, he had met a "ghostly man" in the woods who taught him how to become a wolf, a lion, or a panther if he wished. However, the "ghost" pointed out to him that he would be less likely to be noticed as a wolf, and so it was wolf form that Garnier chose to take. He used his power, he said, to provide food for his wife and children, for they were poor. It is not clear whether the family knew where their meat came from, but Garnier in wolf form had certainly done his best for them. He told of having attacked four children and was generally thought to have made off with several more. He was sentenced by the court to be burned alive on January 18, 1573.

8

Peter Stump and Others

Jean Grenier and Gilles Garnier are only two of the more famous persons tried for werewolfery. Another was Peter Stump.

Stump was known as a good citizen of a small town near Cologne (Cuh-*lone*), Germany. Yet in 1590, he was arrested for a series of murders that had taken place over the past twenty-five years. An English poet later wrote this verse about the case. (I have changed the old-fashioned spelling.)

> A German (called Peter Stump) by charm
> Of an enchanted girdle did much harm,
> Transformed himself into a wolfish shape
> And in a wood did many years escape.

"Much harm" is hardly the way to describe Stump's crimes. He confessed to having murdered his own son as well as so many other people that the number was never known for certain.

Other famous werewolves were the three members of the Gandillon (*Gan*-dee-yawn) family (a sister and brother and the brother's son). They were discovered to be werewolves after the sister's body was found on the spot where a huge wolf without a tail had been killed. The wolf had just attacked two children. The woman's brother and nephew later confessed that all three had been werewolves.

I could go on and on listing the names and dates of famous werewolf trials. However, it is al-

A sixteenth-century woodcut of a hungry werewolf attacking a victim

ready plain that most of these cases are much the same. They are part of a history that goes back at least to the Greek writer Herodotus (Her-*rod*-uh-tus, fifth century B.C.). Herodotus tells us that in his time the people living north of the Black Sea, both Greeks and others, reported that members of a nearby tribe called the Neuri (*Noo*-ree) regularly turned into wolves for a few days each year. Herodotus is careful to say that he doesn't believe the reports himself, but he makes it clear that others did. This may be the earliest written report of werewolves.

They are mentioned by all sorts of writers from that time on. Few claim to have met a werewolf, but many report knowing others who say they have done so. By 1542, it was even recorded that the Sultan of Turkey led his soldiers into the city of Constantinople (Con-stan-ti-*no*-pul) and killed 150 of the monsters. Between Herodotus and the trials mentioned here, there were about two thousand years when many people, if not everyone, believed in werewolves.

What really happened, then? The trials certainly took place. Persons with those names *were* arrested and tried on those dates and in those places. No one doubts the records on those points. But did anyone ever really turn into a wolf? If not, why the legends, the trials, and the histories?

9

Were Werewolves Real?

If you are told over and over that a certain thing is unlucky, and then the unlucky happens to you, you may become very scared indeed. An example of this might be a high-wire artist in a circus, who has performed his dangerous act hundreds of times before the crowds. But if he becomes convinced that he has become "jinxed" or had the "evil eye" put on him, he may actually become too terrified to perform his act or may even fall in the middle of it. In other words, he has ceased to *believe* that he can do it.

In certain societies even today magic is widely believed in. People in those societies have actually died merely because the local magician has cursed them or "pointed the bone" at them. Doctors could find no reason for these deaths except that the individuals had been terrified into *believing* that they would die.

Belief, therefore, is very powerful. It influences what we do and how we do it. Some people may walk blocks out of their way to avoid a house they *believe* is haunted. We laugh at the idea that some of Christopher Columbus's sailors believed that the world was flat and that they might sail over the edge into nothingness. If the great explorer had listened to their fears, he would never have reached the Americas. What fears of ours may be keeping us from even more exciting discoveries?

We may now see that the answer to our question, "Were werewolves real?" may be, "Werewolves were entirely real to those who believed in them."

The captures and trials of Gilles Garnier, Jean Grenier, Peter Stump, and others accused of being werewolves are part of history. The written records are there. In many cases, the so-called werewolves themselves believed that they had taken wolf form when committing their crimes. Like witchcraft (with which it was often confused), werewolfery was utterly real to the terrified people whose children and friends were killed.

The question we ought to ask is probably, "Why were werewolves—and other were-beasts—so widely believed in for so long?"

In the first place, we must consider that in the earliest times men and women lived very closely with animals and the rest of nature. They did not see themselves as very different from the animals who shared the earth with them—the bison, wolf, lion, horse, hawk, and others. Folklore is full of characters such as Old Man Coyote and Elephant Brother. And in tales such as "Little Red Riding Hood," it seems perfectly natural for the wolf to talk, enter a house, and wear clothes. The wolf in "Little Red Riding Hood" is probably the first werewolf most of us hear about, although we don't think of him that way.

Many individuals and tribes had a special kinship with some animal. They thought this special animal (often called a totem) would give protection and advice in bad times and bring luck in good times. People might dress in the skins of their totems, wear masks that looked like them, and imitate their movements. These were magical actions in which the people often felt they *became* the eagle, otter, leopard, wild bull, or other animal. To these people, the idea of a man's turning into an animal and back again was not strange, but simple and natural. Even after such notions are given up for more "civilized" beliefs, they are still whispered about in corners, told in myths or legends, or found in "old wives' tales" and superstitions.

The belief in werewolves and other were-beasts could be partly explained by old memories and tales

In this scene of the Bela Koola Indians, the dancers wear masks of many different animals. The faces on the boats, clothing, and tall carved totem poles also show how human beings, animals, and monsters were mixed together in the Indian's world.

of the long-gone times of animal totems, when men and animals were one.

But a belief as complicated as werewolfery does not always, or even usually, have one simple explanation. In the next chapter I will talk about *some* of the reasons that might have led people to believe in werewolves, even though human beings cannot really change themselves into wolves. We may be right about some of these reasons and wrong about others. We can probably never prove which are which. All we can do is look at the possible reasons for werewolf belief and ask whether some or all of them might be enough to explain werewolves and their relatives.

10

Why Werewolves?

First of all, a large number of were-beasts are, in
their animal form, large and fearsome. We do not
find any were-mice or were-sheep. Instead, the animals chosen are most often wolves, tigers, jaguars,
bears, and so forth. This might be because few of us
wish to be smaller or weaker than we are, but many
have wished to be "as brave as a lion" or "as cunning
as a wolf."

Of all the animals common in Europe in the last
thousand years, the wolf was by far the most feared
by ordinary people. Wolves hunted in groups or
packs, while even the largest bears hunted alone. A
pack of wolves could pull down a full-grown ox or
slash the throats of a whole flock of sheep. The
sound of their howling on cold and lonely nights was
like the wailing of devils and always seemed closer
than it was. Experts on wolves today tell us that wild
wolves almost never attack human beings (unless

their victims are wounded or dying). But the people of those early times had every reason to fear the wolves which cost them so many sheep and cattle and which just *might* (one never knew) turn to man-eating.

Furthermore, many kinds of wild animals sometimes produce an "outlaw"—a single individual that is both stronger and more fearless than others of its kind. Such an animal may become famous for its fierceness, its daring, its cunning, and its ability to es-

cape even the keenest hunters and cleverest traps. "Superwolves" of this kind were certainly not half human and had no ability to disappear. But it must have seemed to those whose flocks and herds suffered from them that only a human mind could be so clever—could seem to *know* exactly where the snare was set and when the huntsmen would loose their dogs.

Likewise, there have been, from time to time, human beings who were so fierce and cruel themselves that they might as well have been wolves. Murder—the killing of human beings by human beings—has always been the most horrible of crimes. Today, we might say that anyone who murders again and again and seems to enjoy it is mad or insane. But there have always been such people, and some of them might well have been called wolves. (In the same way, we call a greedy person a hog or a gossipy person a cat.)

Some murderers or insane persons have actually believed that they committed crimes while in wolf form, although others who were there at the time saw no change in them. Four hundred years ago, however, in the time of Jean Grenier and Gilles Garnier, such stories might well have been believed, and such "confessions" have been taken as proof that werewolves existed. How many "werewolves" who confessed were in reality suffering from a disease of the mind?

There is another reason why some people might have *thought* they could change to wolf form. At least some of those who were tried for witchcraft (of which werewolfery was supposed to be a form) had been rubbing themselves with salves that contained powerful drugs. Many of the things in these salves were the same as those in the recipes used in becoming a werewolf (see pp. 21 and 22). When those who wished to become werewolves really used such drugged salves, they may have convinced themselves that they were werewolves, witches, or whatever else took their fancy. The drugs they used are dangerous, as well as powerful, and their effects are hard to control. Today, some scholars believe that such salves were the reason why many so-called witches, and perhaps werewolves, were so ready to confess to their supposed crimes: they really believed they had committed them.

We have been talking about things people might have feared or believed. But there are two other parts to the werewolf puzzle that have to do with things people could see clearly for themselves, at least in rare cases.

First, it is possible for human beings to be born with fur, like animals. This is very unusual, but it does happen. When it does, it runs in families. For example, in the Canary Islands in the sixteenth century, there lived a family named Gonzales. The father, and at least three children, had light, soft fur over their entire bodies. Their case roused so much

A victim of hypertrichosis

amazement that the king of France, Henry II, had them brought to his court, where he gave them fine clothes and a good living. (Of course, the unfortunate family also had to be stared at and joked about by the king's courtiers. That was unkind, as their condition was not their fault.)

The Gonzaleses were certainly not the only persons in history to suffer this rare condition (which has the long name of hypertrichosis: *hi*-per-tri-*ko*-sis). Such cases get talked about for miles, or even hundreds of miles, around. They might easily be at the root of stories of whole families who were half human, half animal.

Finally, there is a disease called porphyria (por-*feer*-ee-a). Unlike hypertrichosis, which is quite harmless, porphyria is both painful and dangerous. Its exact cause and cure are still unknown. In porphyria, poisonous materials are produced in the body. (These are called porphyrins.) Those who are ill with porphyria may find that light is painful to them. Their skins may become hairy and their teeth may even, in rare cases, turn red. As the disease runs its course, its victims may act very wildly and strangely. They may take to going about only at night (because daylight hurts their eyes), as well as yelling, howling, and doing other things sane people do not do. No one has claimed that victims of porphyria kill people or eat raw meat, but the description fits werewolves so well in every other way that we must wonder what role the disease played in the birth of the werewolf legend. Prophyria even seems to run in families just as werewolfery is often supposed to do.

In the end, no one can say for sure, "*This* was the one cause of belief in werewolfery. But *this* was not." I personally do not believe that human beings ever change into actual animals—wolves, bears, jaguars, or whatever. But that is a long way from being sure I know exactly what made so many people believe in were-beasts for so long.

Human beings *are,* after all, animals. We are all much more like cats or horses or even wolves than we are like stones or trees or flashes of lightning. We know this without thinking about it. So we must not be too surprised if the animal nature sometimes comes out in us as strongly as the human nature. When we act cruel and bloodthirsty (or when we wish to), there is a little bit of the wolf in all of us.

11

The Worst Werewolf
Story of All

The best (or maybe the worst) thing about were-wolves is the scary stories about them. This one has magic in it as well as a werewolf and is one of my favorites.

In the early summer of the year 1840, a Swiss gentleman, Mr. Hellen, went with a friend of his on a walking tour of the Harz Mountains in Germany. For several days they were delighted with the snow-topped peaks, lofty forests, flowery meadows, and cozy villages of the region. Late one afternoon, however, Hellen's friend, whose name was Schiller, slipped on a rock and twisted his ankle. They were far from any town, and night was beginning to fall on the forest. Poor Schiller was unable to walk. He urged Hellen to leave him and go in search of help.

Hellen didn't like the idea of leaving his friend

alone, but there did not seem to be much choice in the matter. He set out through the woods, hoping to find a woodcutter's hut. Once or twice he thought he heard wolves howling, which made him hurry along the path. But he met no one, until suddenly he came to a small clearing in the trees.

The moon was now shining brightly. There in the clearing sat a man who seemed to be in pain. Hellen hurried over and asked whether he could help him. "I'd be most grateful for some help," answered the man. "You see, I fear I have broken my wrist while I was gathering wood for my fire, and I can't seem to bandage it with just one hand."

Hellen did his best for the injured wrist. He explained how he happened to be alone in the forest at night. "Why, how lucky," said his new friend, who gave his name as Wilfred. "My cottage is only a short way from here. We will go there at once, and I will send my daughter back with you. She is young and strong and can help you with your friend. You will both spend the night with us, of course, and whatever we have is yours. But since you are a stranger here," Wilfred went on, "I wonder whether you know what sort of a place you have found yourself in?"

"Why, no," answered Hellen, "only that it must be a lucky place for me to have met such a kind and helpful host."

"Ah," replied Wilfred, laughing, "it is luckier than you think. Any stranger who comes here by moonlight is given two wishes. I know you will say that is nonsense, but I have seen strange things happen in this forest."

"Well," said Hellen, laughing in his turn, "I suppose if I could have my wish, it would be for my dear wife to be here, so that she could see how beautifully I have bandaged your wrist. And the children, too. They would be frightened if she suddenly disappeared and left them alone at home in Frankfort."

"Oh, do you have children?" asked Wilfred. "How fond I am of the dear little things. I hope they are healthy and plump."

"Yes, all three are girls—my sweet Marcella, Christina, and Fredericka. But what's that?" he added in a changed voice, for he heard a loud howling quite nearby.

"A wolf, for sure," replied Wilfred, walking faster. "But have no fear. My cottage is just ahead."

Hellen looked up and indeed saw a neat thatched cottage. A woman and some children were standing at its door. "Great heavens!" he gasped. "That looks like my wife, though I know it cannot be. And my three little girls. Am I mad?"

"No, no," answered Wilfred calmly. "It is only the answer to your wishes. Look, they have seen you and are waving."

Hellen felt as if he were dreaming as he watched his wife and children rush up to him. They should have been hundreds of miles away in their home in Frankfort. "How can this be?" they all cried. "Only a moment ago we were at home in our beds, and now here we are in the middle of this strange forest!"

Hellen could not think what to say, but Wilfred said cheerfully, "Well, well, I think we should all get ourselves to bed. No doubt things will seem clearer in the morning. And now," he added to Hellen, "you must meet my daughter Marguerite."

The bewildered traveler turned and found himself shaking hands with the most beautiful girl he had ever seen. Her dress had a wide border of white fur. Her thick long hair was drawn back under a most becoming ermine cap. Her eyes were green, her teeth were white and even, and Hellen noticed especially that she had delicate fingers, with long, pointed, rosy nails. Yet there was something mysterious about her, something that seemed to speak of wild places, hidden and secret.

Hellen did not give long to these thoughts. Marguerite smiled charmingly and drew the whole family into the cottage. There a simple but very tasty supper was served them. Hellen's wife and children still seemed bewildered by their sudden arrival in this strange place. Soon they were shown into the bedrooms by the kindly Wilfred.

"And now," he said, "we really must do something for your poor friend in the forest. Since my broken wrist is still giving me pain, Marguerite will go with you and help you bring him to the safety of the cottage."

Hellen felt rather guilty at having forgotten his friend during the course of the startling events of the last few hours. Immediately he agreed that he and Marguerite should set out as soon as possible. As they walked together through the moonlit forest, he was more and more drawn by her strange beauty. She moved through the trees as silently and gracefully as some forest creature. He had a hard time keeping up with her.

Then, at last, they reached the spot where Hellen believed he had left his friend only a few hours be-

73

fore. He was surprised to get no answer to his shouts of greeting.

"Where can he be?" he asked Marguerite. "He certainly can't have gone far with an ankle so badly sprained." Only then did he notice the form that lay on the ground by a small clump of bushes.

"Why, there he is!" exclaimed Hellen. "He must have fallen asleep, poor fellow." But when the two rescuers approached closer, they found not a live body, but that of someone mangled and torn almost to pieces.

"Alas!" cried Hellen. "If only I had not left him alone in the forest. What a terrible ending to our holiday! Indeed, I thought I heard wolves howling as I came through the forest with your father. There is nothing for us to do now but to return to the cottage. Wilfred and I will come back in the morning and bury the body."

For some time, as they walked together back toward the cottage, Hellen's thoughts were filled with the sad fate of his friend. Little by little, however, he became aware once more of the beauty of Marguerite. At last, as they came to the clearing where he had first met Wilfred earlier that day, he could contain himself no longer.

"I must be mad," he cried. "Your beauty bewitches

me so that I can think of nothing else. I beg you, Marguerite, let me have just one kiss so that I may remember you forever."

With both surprise and joy, Hellen saw her turn to him and put her arms around him. "And I love you too, believe me. But can you not do better than a kiss? We have again reached the enchanted glade. All you need do is wish, and I can be yours forever."

Forgetting his love for his wife and children, forgetting everything except the glow in Marguerite's green eyes, Hellen gasped, "Yes, yes! The two wishes! You mean that I may have them again?"

"Yes."

"Then I wish, first, that everything that keeps us from being together may be removed. And second, I wish that I may be yours forever." He could hardly believe his good fortune when Marguerite turned and kissed him passionately, then led him once more through the forest.

"You shall see," she said laughingly, "how soon your wishes are granted."

Suddenly, they heard horrifying cries and shrieks for help. "My wife! My children!" cried Hellen. "I must go to them."

He dashed off toward the cottage. Before he could

reach it, the sounds had turned from groans to gurgles to a terrible silence. Entering the door, he found Wilfred bending over the bodies of his wife and children. Wilfred's hands were covered with blood, and his face had the snarling lips and white fangs of a wolf. In his terror, Hellen heard the cottage door close softly behind him.

"And now, my love, you see how easy it is," said Marguerite. "Everything that stood between us is gone and you are mine forever."

Index

About the Author

As a child, Georgess McHargue lived in both New York City and Montana. After graduating *magna cum laude* from Radcliffe, she entered the publishing field and before long began writing her own books. Her deep interests in archaeology, folklore, and the occult often find their way into her books—for example, *The Beasts of Never, The Impossible People,* and *Mummies.* She and her engineer-archaeologist husband, Michael Roberts, live in Groton, Massachusetts, in a 175-year-old house next to a historic graveyard, with a border collie and two cats, but unfortunately no ghosts.